Standing for the King, While in the Spotlight Of the Media

Dr. Jacquelyn Hadnot
Igniting the Fire Publishing

©copyright 2013 Dr. Jacquelyn Hadnot

Standing for the King While in the Spotlight of the Media
Dr. Jacquelyn Hadnot
Published by: Igniting the Fire Publishing
1314 North 38th Street
Kansas City, KS 66102
www.ignitingthefire.net

No part of this publication may be reproduced, stored in a retrieval system, or transmitted, in any form or by any means, electronic, mechanical, photocopying, recording, or otherwise, without the written prior permission of the author.

Unless otherwise noted, all Scripture quotations are taken from King James Version of the Bible.

Scripture quotations marked AMP are taken from The Amplified Bible AMP. The Amplified Bible, Old Testament copyright © 1965, 1987 by the Zondervan Corporation. The Amplified New Testament, copyright © 1954, 1958, 1987 by the Lockman Foundation. Used by permission.

Scripture quotations marked NASB are taken from The New American Standard Bible AMP. Copyright © 1960, 1962, 1963, 1968, 1971, 1972, 1973, 1975, 1977 by the Zondervan Corporation. The Amplified New Testament, copyright © 1954, 1958, 1987 by the Lockman Foundation. Used by permission.

Scripture quotations marked NIV are taken from The New International Version. Copyright © 1973, 1978, 1984 by the International Bible Society. Used by permission.

Cover Design: Dr. Jacquelyn Hadnot
Copyright© 2012 by Dr. Jacquelyn Hadnot
All rights reserved.

Please note that Igniting the Fire's publishing style capitalizes certain pronouns in Scripture that refer to the Father, Son, and Holy Spirit, and may differ from some Bible publishers' styles.

CONTENTS

	Introduction	7
1	Standing for the King, While in the Spotlight of the Media	13
2	Understanding Your Role in the Media	17
3	Check Your Character	29
4	Understanding the Medias Role in Your Ministry	33
5	Ministry Performance Protocols	37
6	Steps to Establish Your Ministry	43
7	Steps to Birthing Your Ministry-*The Ministry Plan*	61
8	Steps to Birthing Your Ministry-*The Marketing Plan*	65
9	Steps to Creating the Budget	69
10	Addressing Your Personal Financial Situation	72
11	How to Get Distribution!	75
12	The Budget & Allocation of Funds	79
13	Getting Your Music on the Radio?	83
14	Radio Stations That Will Play Your Music	85
15	How to Get Your Music on Pandora Internet Radio	91
16	14 Ways to Promote Your Music Online	95
17	Want a Radio Interview?	101
18	How to Prepare for TV	103
19	How to Get Coverage In Print Media	107
20	Got A Press Kit? What's a Press Kit?	111
21	Let the Vision Speak	115
22	Are Your Ready to Minister for the King?	119
	Appendix	125
	About the Author	129
	Others Books by Dr. Jacquie	131
	Space for Notes	133
	Kingdom Media Foundation	137

Standing for the King, While in the Spotlight of the Media

Standing for the King, While in the Spotlight of the Media

Dr. Jacquelyn Hadnot
Igniting the Fire Publishing

Standing for the King, While in the Spotlight of the Media

Introduction

After being in the eye of the media for several years and teaching at the Kingdom Music Festival for several years, the Lord dropped in my spirit to put together a book that outlines the information and impartations that I have received over the years.

I have ministered to wide-eyed individuals for years on the subject of the media promoting your ministry gifts. There is a way to promote your gift without the added pressure of subjecting yourself to the pains and stains of a sometimes-godless media system. You can take your gift to the nations without "whoring" yourself to the nations.

I firmly believe that as Kingdom builders and agents of change, we can access the seven cultural mountains and bring about a paradigm shift that sets the world on its face and on fire for the King of Kings. I believe that we can be IN the world and not OF the world. I also believe that if we stand in the face of a godless media system with an uncompromising message of Jesus Christ, that we can and will make a difference. Have you ever complained about the movies and television shows that portray our Lord as small and insignificant? If we had more Christian writers and directors, we would set the standard for what is served to the public. What about record labels that allow the worst lyrical content to come from their labels? If Christians were at the helm of these companies, again we would set the standard for what is produced. Finally, what about radio stations who play the vile music that record labels produce? Again, if we served as radio station owners, operators, music directors and radio announcers, we could lift up a standard in the radio industry. It is time to raise the bar in the media industry and as Believers; it is time that we take this cultural mountain for the King of Kings.

Who is the King of Glory? The Lord strong and mighty, the Lord mighty in battle. He is ready to do battle on your behalf. Your requirement, stand and see Him do a great work in you, through you and for you. Your assignment if you decide to accept it - stand in the spotlight of the media while you stand for the King of Kings.

What qualifies me to write this book? My 30 years as a successful entrepreneur, accountant and financial adviser. The fact that I have owned an online radio station for five years. The fact that we own and operate ITF Television and host a weekly show on ION Television with potential viewers well into the millions. Is it the fact that we have produced music since 2005 for and with artists around the country?

Whatever the case, I believe that it is time to take my years in the spotlight of the media and share it with you in hopes of shedding light on the subject for which you purchased this book.

As you stand in the midst of the spotlight of the media, I know that the information in this book will be invaluable to help you stand and withstand the pressures associated with the notoriety, publicity, and the like.

The information included in this book is practical advice for the up and coming ministry gift. You are a ministry gift that has been blessed with a great ability that the Lord desires to use for the building of His Kingdom. "Go ye" into the cultural mountains of the media and take a message of hope to a dying world.

Finally, in this book I will cover several aspects of your ministry, the intrinsic (internal) and extrinsic (external). You must know how to carry yourself from a spiritual, mental, emotional and financial perspective. You MUST have balance in every area if you are going to have the longevity that is required to be a Kingdom Priest.

I have had the sad misfortune of counseling individuals that had a lofty ideology when it came to ministry, music and the media. I recall a minister saying, "When I got into ministry, I thought it was going to be glamorous." I laughed and replied, "Have you seen the glamour yet?" If you are getting into this for the glitz and glamour, you are in for a big surprise. This is a race for the Kingdom prize and it is not given to the swift or strongest singer, lyricist, rapper, artist, musician, writer or businessperson, it is given to the one who endures to the end. Can you endure? Do you have the strength to endure?

Throw away your big dreams of a Jay-Z like Christian Rap career (*you cannot afford the price he paid*) and PICK UP YOUR CROSS. Burn your lofty ideas of fame and fortune and PICK UP YOUR CROSS and follow Christ and He will exalt you in your due season.

Let's get down to the business of birthing your ministry for the King and for the Kingdom.

Chapter 1

Standing for the King, While in the Spotlight of the Media

IT'S GOT TO BE A GOD THING!

The Lord has birthed within you a desire to minister in the areas of music, dance, teaching, preaching or other areas of ministry. Within the area of your calling are the methods of media: radio, television, film or other forms of broadcasting or communication. The vision God has for your life is awesome and this is just the beginning of where He wants to take you. In order to be ready for the destiny that is set before you, you must walk through your season of preparation.

In order to get to the fullness of God's plan and purpose for your life you must be equipped with essential information that is vital to the growth and success of the ministry.

It is my prayer that you will find the steps below helpful in assisting you in *Standing for the King, While in the Spotlight of the Media.*

The Bible tells us to seek Godly counsel and I pray that the Lord leads you as He has lead me to gather the necessary information to walk in the spotlight of the media in a manner that will give Him glory.

I firmly believe that as Christians we can promote the businesses or ministries that God has blessed us with and do so while ***promoting without pride.*** Remember, God said that He would not share His glory without anyone. *I am the LORD: that is my name: and **my glory** will I not give to another, neither my praise to graven images* (Isaiah 42:8).

> *Even every one that is called by my name: for I have created him for **my glory**, I have formed him; yea, I have made him* (Isaiah 43:7).

> *For mine own sake, even for mine own sake, will I do it: for how should my name be polluted? And I will not give **my glory** unto another* (Isaiah 48:11).

> *If ye will not hear, and if ye will not lay it*

*to heart, to give **glory unto my name**, saith the LORD of hosts, I will even send a curse upon you, and I will curse your blessings: yea, I have cursed them already, because ye do not lay it to heart.* (Malachi 2:2)

The King will not share His glory with anyone and that includes you. He is sharing His gifts with you and that should be more than enough. If you want your ministry to prosper, recognize when the enemy is trying to insert the spirit of pride into your heart. It will shut your destiny down and doors will close and remain closed until you address this deadly enemy of your destiny. In other words, you must understand your role in the media.

Chapter 2

Understanding Your Role in the Media

It is vital to understand your role in the media. Many Believers have launched out into the spotlight of the media and got lost amidst the glitch and glamour of its trappings. Many well-meaning artists, musicians, actors and the like have been thrust into the spotlight and along the way, forgot their God given assignment. The result, they became part and parcel of the very medium they were sent in the set a standard. Lights, cameras, action! As the lights blaze and the cameras roll, it is often easy to forget the reason for your elevation if you are not rooted and grounded on a firm foundation - Jesus Christ.

I recall the first year of my thrust into the lights of the media. It was not an easy journey because it was an area I was not accustomed. The music tours, traveling and music awards became an instrument of the enemy. He devised a plan to manipulate me into a position of pride. The Lord in His infinite wisdom put a check in my spirit that led me to the threshing floor of repentance. The Lord checked me early in my ministry that was surrounded by the media.

Unfortunately, many people receive that check in their spirit, but how many heed the voice of the Lord and destroy the spirit of pride, envy, jealousy and the like? For many they travel the road of success in the eyes of man, while failing in the eyes of the Lord. Yes, you will have a modicum of success in the world, but what about the real success that the King wants to give you if only you follow His directives and root your gifts, talents and ministry in Him. It is one thing to say that we give it all to Him, but it is an entirely different thing to give it to Him without the stench of pride and vainglory.

One thing is for sure, the minute you are thrust into the spotlight, is the moment when your core values will be tested, your foundation will be tried and your hunger for acceptance and recognition may be enticed. Why? With each tests, the enemy will attempt to insert his demonic manipulations into the plan.

Your role in the spotlight of the media is simple:

To Give God Glory. If you are going to give Him glory there are steps that are necessary to ensure that He is getting the glory and not you. I like to call them caution steps: You must:

- Recognize that it is not you doing the work; it is the Lord working through you.

- Bring your decisions before the throne.

- Never allow secular handlers, managers, producers, agents to handle the "baby" God has given you.

- Never allow the media to "whore" out your gifts simply to get appearances on radio, television or other mediums.

- Never reduce your gift to a paycheck; this will make you a hireling.

Standing for the King, While in the Spotlight of the Media

- Don't get in a hurry to launch your "career" and miss the season of preparation that is vital for your stability.

- Never make your ministry gift about money. Opportunities may be presented to you that open more doors of favor that money cannot buy.

- Seek wise counsel before signing or negotiating contracts.

- Whenever accolades and recognition are thrust at you, remember behind every compliment lies the opportunity for the enemy to insert pride and cause your destiny to be hindered and held back. Therefore, pray against and destroy the spirit of pride because it is lurking out there to shut you down.

- Never allow anyone to decide what assignments to accept. Consult God FIRST!

- Never kick doors open in order to drag your gift in the room for others to see. Remember, it is the Lord's gift and your gift will make room for you. Psalm 127:1 says, *"Unless the LORD builds the house, those who built it labor in vain."*

- Learn to discern the spirits in operation in the culture of entertainment. Not everyone ushering you to a door of opportunity is there in your best interest. Again, know what spirits are in operation.

- Stay abreast of currents trends and changes in the media. Never try to flow in any system with out dated information. There are many books out there to help you stay abreast of the industry. Always be in a position to learn.

- As much as possible, travel with your spouse if you are married. This keeps the road temptations (groupies) out of your face. And it keeps your home happy.

- Repent of your past or hidden sins as soon as they are revealed to you. Un-confessed sin has a way of coming back to bite you in the behind. If you have a problem with pornography, it will surface when you are in a hotel alone with 200 porn channels.

- Minister TO the King before you minister FOR the King. The worst thing you can do is go out before people without spending quality time with the Lord. You will go from MINISTERING to PERFORMING in one fatal step. It will be a misstep that will cost you. I have heard many people trying to minister from a place of emptiness and it shows.

➢ Stay in the Word of God. It is impossible to minister for the King when you don't know what the King desires.

➢ **PRAY, PRAY, PRAY.** Prayer is the key to hearing the voice of the Lord for His will for the vision of the ministry He has given you. As you are seeking the Lord, keep a pen and paper handy and write down all that the Lord pours into you. God gives three answers: YES, NO or WAIT. *1 Thessalonians 5:17-18 tells us pray without ceasing. In every thing, give thanks: for this is the will of God in Christ Jesus* *concerning you.* If you don't **PRAY,** you could become **PREY**!

Your role in the arena of media is vital to the Kingdom agenda. It is through you that the message of the King and the Kingdom will be spread. Therefore, you must be alert in every area that pertains to your ministry. You cannot be in everything, but you can be aware of many things. When you find an area that you are unfamiliar with, align yourself with individuals that are likeminded and Christ-minded to strengthen you where you are weak. For example, if you are unfamiliar with the tax laws, hire an accountant to help you navigate through the tax laws that pertain to your ministry. Just because you are in ministry does not mean you are exempt from federal, state or local taxes. Don't make the mistake of getting behind before you get ahead.

Look at many of the artists, actors and other entertainers who have fallen because of their lack of tax knowledge. Don't become a victim of lack of knowledge because people perish for lack of knowledge. Finally, PRAY! I can't stress the need for prayer enough. Prayer will keep you when nothing else will.

The ministry gift God has given you is only as effective as the vessel in which it is housed. The gifts you possess are with you regardless of whether you live right, walk right and love right. In other words, it is yours even if you never repent of a single sin in your life. However, that doesn't mean that you will reach your full potential. God gave you the gifts and He may not take them back, but that doesn't mean that He has to bless them. *"For the gifts and calling of God are without repentance"* (Romans 11:29).

Standing for the King, While in the Spotlight of the Media

Watch your character.

Standing for the King, While in the Spotlight of the Media

Chapter 3

Check Your Character

I would like to begin this chapter with one of the most important statements you will ever read:

Your gifts and talents will get you to the top, but your character and integrity will keep you there.

Many people have "made it" in the entertainment industry, but do you ever wonder why many of them failed? Could it be their character? Could it be the lack of integrity?

Your character is one of the most important

aspects of your ministry. Without character, you may make it to the "top" but I assure you your rise will be short lived. Character and integrity are vital to your ability to stand and withstand. Stand in the face of adversity, trials and tribulation. Withstand against the wiles, tricks, traps and manipulations of the devil.

What is character? Character is your public reputation. **What is integrity?** Integrity is the possession of firm principles: the quality of possessing and steadfastly adhering to high moral principles or professional standards.

Without character and integrity, you will fall for anything and anyone. Without character and integrity, you will be prey for whatever the enemy throws your way. Without character and integrity, you will be "whored out" as soon as your name hit's the streets. Every circuit manager, promoter or producer will know your name and it won't be a name that stands for anything. If you start your ministry career out with a bad name or reputation, it will follow you like a bad odor. Again, your gifts and talent will get you through the door, but it is your character and integrity that will keep the Lord's hand on your ministry back and the media seeking you out.

Learn to walk in the **Ischus** power of God (*Is chus is Greek for strength. From health to moral endowment. Applied capacity, ability to perform*). Walk in integrity in every area of your life and ministry. It is a lifestyle choice.

Standing for the King, While in the Spotlight of the Media

Chapter 4

Understanding the Medias Role in Your Ministry

It is important that you understand the role of the media as it pertains to your ministry. Understand that the media is not designed to be your friend. One day the media will sing your praises and the next, crucify him. The media is a tool to spread the message of Jesus Christ to a dying world. The media is a tool by which we take the airwaves by force. A spiritual striving to bring people out of darkness and into the knowledge that will set them free. It is also a tool to challenge the world to become more than the sum of its parts. In other words, stop being an instrument of evil and become an agent of and for change. As Kingdom men and women, it is our mandate to access the media and bring about change. It is not media that should change us; we should be changing the face of media. I believe that through vehicles like the Kingdom Media Festival, we can bring awareness to the mechanics of the media and thereby begin to effect change within its hallowed walls and secret societies.

In order to accomplish this monumental task, we must be ready for whatever is thrown at us. We must not succumb to the tricks, traps and shares of a godless media system. We cannot remain behind the walls of Christian television, radio and print media if we are going to reach the lost.

We must be ready, willing and able to reach the masses that are NOT reading Christian magazines, watching Christian television, or listening to Christian radio. We must be ready to take our message of hope and healing wherever and whenever the opportunity presents itself. But we can't do it if we are not ready.

We must know how to flow in whatever vein, system and structure we are called. We are not simply called to minister to other Believers; we are called to the nations. Our call to reach the nations will include going into the media and setting a standard.

Therefore, our role in the media is to be an agent of and for change and the role of media in your ministry is to be the tool that takes your message to the world. You are not going in to make friends, you are being sent in to set a standard, a Kingdom standard with a Kingdom agenda.

In order to accomplish this enormous task, there are things that you must know. These things are vital to your survival, assignment and advancement. You cannot go into the enemy's territory without the necessary ammunition to avoid his traps and snares. You must be ready to defeat the tricks, traps and snares if you are to advance for the Kingdom.

You are a kingdom warrior with a kingdom assignment that will bring glory to the kingdom of our God.

Chapter 5

Ministry Performance Protocols

Before we go into the areas that guide you into the spotlight of ministry, we must address the protocols of ministry. Without them, you will end up being just another performer and not a Kingdom Builder.

When I am looking for individuals to minister on one of our platforms such as the Life in the Spirit Awards, The Exchange Television Talk Show or one of our radio broadcasts, I don't look for great singers, actors, or musicians, I look for anointed ministers that know how to adhere to protocols and set a standard of excellence.

What is a protocol? A protocol is:

- The rules or conventions of correct behavior on official or ceremonial occasions.

- Code of conduct: the rules of correct or appropriate behavior of a group, organization, or profession.

What are the protocols that are valuable if you want to get the first call and even a return call? Consider this your Code of Conduct checklist. If you are lacking in any of the following areas, chances are you are not getting the invitations that you desire. Your adherence to the following protocols will determine whether you are ready for ministry on the next level. It will also determine what promoters, booking agents, pastors, television, radio or other industry decision makers see in you and hear about you.

MINISTRY PROTOCOLS

Stay until the end:

When ministering at a church or ministry, avoid leaving before the end of the event. Nothing irritates leadership more than artists or musicians who perform and then leave. I make it a policy to note individuals who perform and then leave on a regular basis. Why? Because I won't call them to be a part of any events, we sponsor. How will you hear the Word of God if you don't sit under the Word? There may be a time when leaving is unavoidable, but make sure to tell the person in charge that you will have to leave.

Be in position:

Make sure that you are in place at the start of the event. The schedule might change and you won't be aware of the changes and might miss your opportunity to minister for the King.

Check your wardrobe:

Be sure to check your wardrobe to ensure that you don't have a wardrobe malfunction. Always carry extra items that might be vital to your ability to minister unhindered.

Be mindful of time:

Always be mindful of your performance time. There is nothing more annoying than someone who has exceeded his time. It throws the schedule off and may cause another performer to miss his opportunity. Also, this kind of behavior will ensure that you won't be asked back.

No shameful promotions:

When it is your time to minister, please don't spend it "promoting" your project or your ministry. Set up a vendor booth and use it as a platform to promote your project.

When you adhere to the protocols of the house, it will go along way in ensuring that you are walking in the spirit of excellence.

Standing for the King, While in the Spotlight of the Media

Chapter 6

Steps to Establish Your Ministry

One of the worst things you can do to your ministry is to start out messy. Regardless of whether it is a ministry, business or hobby, all things must be done decent and in order. The same is true with your ministry. You must establish order in your ministry from day one. Otherwise, you are destined to fail.

Here are some steps to take in order to establish your ministry. The bible tells us to write the vision and make it plain so that whoever reads it can run with it. You must have clear and concise instructions in order to run with the vision that is before you.

I am including these vital steps so that you won't succumb to the pressures of the world's system and birth an unprepared "baby" and later destroy it. There's nothing worse than becoming a spectacle in the spotlight of the media. Look at actors, artists and ministers that have fallen due to poor financial management. Some have even gone to prison. If you follow these steps, it won't happen to you. Remember, this book is designed to make sure you are balanced in every area before you step into the spotlight. Because once you are there, it is hard to shut down the lights in order to get your affairs straight.

STEP 1

PRAY, PRAY, PRAY. Prayer is the key to hearing the voice of the Lord for His will for the vision of the ministry He has given you. As you are seeking the Lord, keep a pen and paper handy and write down all that the Lord pours into you. God gives three answers: YES, NO and WAIT. *1 Thessalonians 5:17-18 pray without ceasing. In every thing, give thanks: for this is the will of God in Christ Jesus concerning you.* **If you don't PRAY, you could become PREY!**

STEP 2

Choose a business structure. For example, Sole Proprietorship, General Partnership, Corporation, Limited Liability Company (LLC) or Non Profit Organization. The business structure will determine the tax liabilities of your ministry's revenues.

STEP 3

File a fictitious ministry name by going to your Secretary of State Office. (Make sure you choose at least 3 names for your ministry just in case the others are taken.) The Secretary of State will also file your business structure application if you choose a Partnership, Corporation or Limited Liability Company when you are ready.

STEP 4

Trademark your ministry name. After you have created a fictitious ministry name and registered it, go a step further and have it trademarked.

STEP 5

Apply for a business license through your local City Hall. Filing fees may vary depending on your city requirements.

STEP 6

Apply for a Federal Tax Identification Number (EIN). A Federal Identification Number is the equivalent of a social security number for your business or ministry entity. You can apply for this online at www.irs.gov.

STEP 7

Open a separate bank account for your ministry in the company name. Don't mix your personal monies with your ministry funds. (The IRS frowns on this activity known as co-mingling.)

STEP 8

Have business cards and letterhead professionally printed. Please don't handwrite your cards or letterhead. That's really ghetto! Also, consider designing a company brochure with information on the company's services. Find yourself a good printer or contact your local Kinko's or Office Depot.

STEP 9

Research and hire a team of professionals. Before you even think about signing any contracts as an artist, minister, musician you need to hire a consultant and an entertainment lawyer. A qualified attorney will set your legal matters in order. Artist agreements and producer agreements can be complex and binding.

STEP 10

The bible says to study to show yourself approved unto God. If you plan to give God your best – STUDY. Starting out, the responsibility is on you to get information that attorneys and experts learn through years of education and experience. Understanding manufacturing, distribution, marketing, recording, advertising and promoting are crucial to your success.

STEP 11

Write the vision and make it plain. *And the LORD answered me, and said, write the vision, and make it plain upon tables, that he may run that reads it (Habakkuk 2:2).* A good vision plan is crucial. A good plan must include the following: a detailed narrative outlining the vision step by step, a marketing plan, and a budget detailing the costs for marketing, promotions, advertising, production, travel, etc. Your personal financial situation must also be addressed during your planning sessions. This should be done separately so that you don't co-mingling funds or information. You can start your ministry on a shoestring budget, but you should not start out deep in debt. Debt reduction is vital to the longevity of your ministry. The bible says to *owe no man anything except to love Him.*

STEP 12

Stay Focused and Prioritize. Don't get lazy when things aren't going the way you want them to go. Through every test is a testimony of how God brought you through. You must have faith for your faith to birth this vision. Read Jeremiah 29:11-13**:** ***For I know the thoughts that I think toward you, saith the LORD, thoughts of peace, and not of evil, to give you an expected end. Then shall ye call upon me, and ye shall go and pray unto me, and I will hearken unto you. And ye shall seek me, and find me, when ye shall search for me with all your heart.***

Your ability to prioritize will go along way in helping you stay focused. Without setting priorities, your vision will be scattered and tattered. Dr. Myles Monroe writes in his book, Kingdom Principles, *"When your priorities are correct, you preserve and protect your life. Correct priority is the principle of progress because when you establish your priority according to your purpose and goals then your progress is guaranteed."*

STEP 13

Consider taking a class on small ministry or business management at your local college.

STEP 14

Establish a telephone line with a professional voice mail or answering service. Nothing turns people off more than unprofessional telephone etiquette or lack thereof. Try using SKYPE or FREE CONFERENCE CALL.COM. You will have an independent number for your ministry or business that is professional and stores messages.

STEP 15

Establish a relationship with an accountant or financial adviser to keep the books of the ministry. Nothing kills a vision faster than falling out of favor with Caesar (IRS). Remember Jesus said, *Render therefore unto Caesar the things which are Caesar's; and unto God the things that are God's (Matthew 22:21).*

STEP 16

As the ministry begins to make a profit open a separate bank tax account to accumulate the ministry income taxes. When it is time to pay your taxes whether it is monthly, quarterly or annually the money will be there and you won't find yourself in a strain robbing Peter to pay Paul (Caesar.) Your accountant will advise you when you have reached this level. Go back and read Matthew 22:21. *NOTE: Your tax accountant will instruct you on the tax ramifications of your ministry's organizational structure. STEP #2.*

STEP 17

Invest in books on the music industry. Stay abreast of the ever-changing industry as it relates to your ministry. Nothing hurts a ministry more than a lack of information. People perish for a lack of knowledge and so will your ministry.

STEP 18

When in doubt – pray and seek Godly counsel. Surround yourself with positive people. Nothing can kill a dream faster than negative, playa hating friends. God as given you the vision and you are the only one that will bring it to fruition. Hangers on are often there to distract you and keep your focus off of God and His plan for your life. If this is your dream – walk it as well as talk it. You must live, breath and pray this vision into existence. Seek Godly counsel for the answers. Counsel from man is important, but counsel from God is vital.

> *And they said unto him, Ask counsel, we pray thee, of God, that we may know whether our way which we go shall be prosperous. (Judges 18:5)*

> *And the children of Israel arose, and went up to the house of God, and asked counsel of God. (Judges 20:18)*
> *We took sweet counsel together, and walked unto the house of God in company. (Psalm 55:14)*

> *But seek ye first the kingdom of God, and his righteousness; and all these things shall be added unto you. (Matthew 6:33)*

STEP 19

Don't be over zealous!! Start slowly. Pace

yourself and don't add too many artists too fast. Not everyone that has a desire to sing has the call on their life to be professional singers or ministers of the gospel. Remember your friends may not see the vision in the beginning, but just wait until there are physical signs of life in the ministry, they will want to jump on board and get a record deal. Everyone wants to be a part of something great. They may not help you when things are down, but they will want to be there when things are going well. The Lord spoke these words to me one afternoon as I was leaving the ministry because I was hurt because I had to close the food pantry three days of the week due to lack of help. The Lord said, *"No one wants to help you now in the ministry, but there will come a day when they want to help you because of who you are."* I started crying because I didn't understand. What I didn't really understand was WHO I AM IN CHRIST. People see you where you are at this moment, but Christ Jesus sees you down the road. He sees where he is taking you – your expected end. The bottom line is this – ask the Lord to give you the people He wants to be signed to your ministry. You never know you just might be the only artist\minister He signs because He has your undivided attention and you have His.

STEP 20

PRAY, PRAY, PRAY. Prayer is the key to hearing the voice of the Lord for His will for the vision of a ministry He has given you. As you are seeking the Lord, keep a pen and paper and write down all that the Lord pours into you. Pray with ceasing. *James 5:16b says the effectual* ***(effective, powerful)*** *fervent* ***(passionate,***

burning) *prayer of a righteous man avails **(rewards, benefits)** much.* Be consistent with God don't be wishy-washy. Be intimate with God and seek His face for His will for your life, or ministry. Remember God has a wonderful plan for you, but you must do everything decent and in order because the Lord does not dwell in the midst of confusion.

<u>All roads must lead to Jesus.</u> God has already ordered every step you take, so why not ask Him for directions. After all, He designed the road and He knows the expected end.

Stay Christ Centered throughout the assignment that He has you on and He will lead and guide you. The Word says to trust in the Lord. Do you trust in Him?

As for God, his way is perfect; the word of the LORD is tried: he is a buckler to all them that trust in him. (2 Samuel 22:31)

Offer the sacrifices of righteousness, and put your trust in the LORD. (Psalm 4:5)

In the LORD put I my trust: how say ye to my soul, Flee as a bird to your mountain? (Psalm 11:1)

The LORD is my rock, and my fortress, and my deliverer; my God, my strength, in whom I will trust; my buckler, and the horn of my salvation, and my high tower. (Psalm 18:2)

Commit thy way unto the LORD; trust also in him; and he shall bring it to pass. (Psalm 37:5)

But it is good for me to draw near to God: I have put my trust in the Lord GOD, that I may declare all thy works. (Psalm 73:28)

Trust in the LORD with all thine heart; and lean not unto thine own understanding. (Proverbs 3:5)

Finally, a word on prosperity, everyone wants to be prosperous, but very few truly understand what it means to be prosperous.

The Word of God says in 3 John 1:2 *Beloved, I wish above all things that your may prosper and be in health, even as thy soul prospers.*

Your soul must prosper in the Lord and with prosperity in Him all the other things will be given to you. Seek God first.

Standing for the King, While in the Spotlight of the Media

Chapter 7

Steps to Birthing Your Ministry
The Ministry Plan

The following information is required to create an effective ministry or business plan. The ministry or business plan will vary from industry to industry. An effective written plan is mandatory if you are seeking financing to capitalize your ministry. You may not require financing for your ministry today, but in the event it is needed, these are the necessary steps to help you when the time comes. You must write the vision and make it plain so that the lending institution is clear on your objectives..

Executive Summary

The Company
    Company History
    Present Situation
    Financial Statements
    Company Goals

The Product or Service
    Product or Service Description
    Product or Service Features
    Product or Service Line

Operations and Production
    Production Strategy and Requirements
    Distribution Strategy
    Other Supporting Data

Management
    Management Team and Qualifications
    Organizational Structure
    People/Talent to Be Hired
    Outside Services
    Compensation Summary

Financial Projections
    Cash Flow Projections
    Profit and Loss Projections
Appendix
    Footnotes
    Executive Resumes
    Letters of Reference
    Legal Documents & Other

As you begin organizing your information for your ministry plan, please keep in mind that you may require the services of a financial adviser/accountant for the more detailed aspects of the plan. Once you have compiled the necessary information, seek the advise of a business adviser to ensure your plan meets the financial institutions requirements. There is nothing worse than presenting a poorly written plan. Invest in an hour of consultation services to ensure your plan is sound. Invest in yourself so that others will want to also.

Standing for the King, While in the Spotlight of the Media

Chapter 8

Steps to Birthing Your Ministry
The Marketing Plan

Now that you have a product, how will you get it into the hands of the buying public? You will need more than the trunk or back seat of your car.

An effective marketing plan is vital to the success of your music product. It does not matter whether you are shopping a major distribution deal or going with independent distribution, a marketing plan is your road map to SALES.

Your marketing analysis requires regular review in order to stay abreast of trends and tracking effectiveness of your marketing and promotions avenues.

Marketing Analysis
    Introduction
    Customer Identification

The Industry
    Size

The Competition
    Main Competitors

Marketing Plan
    Market Segment
    Reaching Customers

Marketing and Promotions
    Sales Locations Retail Stores
    Online Sales Locations
    Radio Air Play – Offline Stations
    Radio Air Play – Online Stations
    Print Media
    Online Media

Television Appearances
Promotional Web Sites
Calendar of Events
Awards and Recognitions
Chart Toppers
CD Reviews

One Sheet
The overview of your product or vision. See chapter 11.

This is an outline of a marketing plan. By following this outline, it should help you compile the necessary information to build an effective, results producing marketing plan.

Standing for the King, While in the Spotlight of the Media

Chapter 9

Steps to Creating the Budget

The budget is the key to effective use of your cash flow. Without a budget it like "spitting in the wind," something is bound to blow back at you. Your budget must possess several areas if it is to encompass an effective strategy of maintaining a positive cash flow. It does not matter if you have a shoestring budget or unlimited capital, a budget will ensure that:

1. Funds are distributed to key areas.
2. You are not overspending without any real effectiveness.

3. You cover the vital areas involved with a successful project.
4. You are a wise steward of what God has entrusted to you.
5. Funds are targeted to key areas for maximum effectiveness.

I have identified 5 areas necessary for effective budgeting and allocation of funds in order to complete your project. It doesn't matter what you are called to do, a budget is vital for it's success. Make adjustments to the budget items below to fit your needs. This budget has been designed to the music industry.

STUDIO BUDGET
Producer Advance Fee
Studio Time
Lead vocals
Background vocals
Overdubs
Mastering
Misc. Time

DUPLICATION BUDGET
Cover Design
Graphic Artist
Photography
CD Duplication\Replication

TALENT COST
Lead Musicians
Musicians (4)
Overdubs
Background Singers
Choir
Lead Singers
Engineer

MARKETING BUDGET
Press Release
Traditional Press Kits
Electronic Press Kit
TV Commercials
Radio Commercials
Website Design
Social Media Advertising (Facebook, etc.)
Posters\Flyers\Postcards
Street Team (when necessary)
Release\Launch Party

TOURING BUDGET
Hotels
Vehicles
Food
Clothing
Travel (airline, bus, etc.)

Regardless of your area of ministry, you will have to hit the road at some point. So be prepared to establish a budget to avoid the pitfalls of running out of money before you complete the tour. There is a budget sheet in the Appendix section.

Chapter 10

Addressing Your Personal Financial Situation
Financial Planning Made Easy
You Need a Budget Too

DEBT FREE IS THE WAY TO BE!! Debt free is not impossible, it can be a reality. My husband and I did it when God began to birth the ministry and so can you if you are determined to move to another level in ministry, business, and in God.

Did you know that there are more than 2,350 verses in the Bible that speak about money and possessions? Other than love, Jesus talked about money and possessions more than any other subject. HUM?

Review your information with an accountant to assist you in determining your financial situation. Never go into a venture under capitalized or robbing Peter to pay Paul. Take a realistic look at your financial situation by establishing a budget to move you into a debt free status.

Gather all your bills and establish balances owed, and the length of time it will take you to pay off the debt.

Remember, it is vital that as you move into this new level in your life that you avoid making new debt at all cost.

Chapter 11

How to Get Distribution!

Most new artists believe that a distributor is the pipeline to the people. Theoretically, it is, but in practice, it is not. A distribution company is only as good as the record company's promotional capacity. Yes, it is important to get your music in stores, but it is much more important to get your MUSIC OUT of that store and into the hands of listeners. A distributor can only try to convince a retail store to take your music, book, DVD or other project. To secure shelf space you or your label will need to present a strong marketing strategy so that the retailer is confident that it can sell your project.

Stores are saturated with product. Stores such as Wal-Mart are not in the business of providing shelf space for a project that is not moving. What does a retailer look for when it is considering placing your project in it's store?

Radio Play

A CD single being worked at radio stations and getting spins, might be enough to convince a store in that neighborhood to take your record. The amount of demand for the record will determine the amount of units the store takes.

Retail Price and Positioning

Visibility in a record store is everything! If you were to buy an "end cap" (those displays at the end of an aisle), or a month on a listening station, or rack display, this is enough to attract the attention of a store. However, it has become increasingly competitive even when you pay for this!

Touring

Playing live shows can help create a demand for a CD and this of course is key. Initially, you might have to establish tour dates on your own until you can secure a booking agent.

One Sheet

Every artist needs a "one sheet" - a hand out sheet with bullet points outlining their marketing strategies and promotional commitments. The "one sheet" gives an overview of your project without the hassle of loads of paper.

Standing for the King, While in the Spotlight of the Media

Chapter 12

The Budget & Allocation of Funds

Key Question: Where will I get the money to birth the project? Where God has given vision, He will provide provision.

Funding sources are not as distant as you might think. If your budget requirements are $25,000 from start to finish based on your expense budget, begin developing a list of possible funding sources.

Below is a list of possible funding sources to utilize to avoid as much debt as possible.

1. Consider a part-time job. All funds from the additional job will be set aside in an interest bearing account for the project.

2. By starting a ministry and incorporating your first advantage is that you can enlist the help of friends and relatives by offering them a percentage of the company's stock. Not stock trading on the open market but as a privately held corporation. Seek a financial adviser for more information

3. Sell unwanted items and place the money in an interest bearing account.

4. When possible ask the band members (if applicable) to each contribute a designated amount to the project. Again, the funds will be placed in an interest bearing account.

5. If you have a savings account, certificates of deposit or other interest bearing accounts, consider borrowing against it. This will do two things for you: (a) it will establish credit for you. (b) It will allow you to use the lending institutions money instead of your own. © By using your own funds to secure the loan, you will get a better interest rate.

6. Keep in mind that there are other ways to generate funds for your project. Ask the Lord to reveal His desire for your steps. Remember your steps are ordered by God.

Standing for the King, While in the Spotlight of the Media

Chapter 13

Getting Your Music on the Radio?

How do you get your music on the radio?

Generally speaking, to get your music played on the radio, the music or program directors of the stations you want your music to be played on need to approve it. So, it is a good idea to try to get to know music and program directors of radio stations to find out what their policies are for accepting music.

Commercial stations tend to get their music

directly from the labels or on compilations put out by large distributors. There are some commercial stations that are willing to accept music from small indie labels, but they tend to be in the minority. Noncommercial stations, and college stations in particular are generally more flexible about accepting new music, since they are not (usually) in the business of competing for listeners, so they are free to present a diverse mix of music to their audiences. Many non-comms and college stations feature some sort of live showcase of new music, which is another opportunity for getting your music on the air.

In general, the best thing to do is to get to know the music and program directors at the stations that you want your music to be played on. If possible, visit the stations to get an idea of how they're run.[1]

Chapter 14

Radio Stations That Will Play Your Music

Here is a brief list of radio stations that will play your music. For a more detailed list, visit the Indie Bible[2].

WAAW Shout 94.7 FM
PO Box 940, Aiken, SC 29802
PH: 803-649-6405 FX: 803-641-8844
Harry Hughes hhughes@waaw947.fm
www.waaw947.fm
Serving to the edification of the Body of Christ and community building by providing sound ministry, Gospel music and in formation to masses through daily talk programs and business and community partnerships. Audio materials must be submitted in one of the following formats: WAV, MP3 or WMA. (For proprietary formats â€" please consult with WAAW). Audio materials may be

submitted on the following media: CD, data DVD, flash drives and other various memory cards. We recommend that you send files through "Yousendit."

New Driven Radio - WBCX
PH: 770-538-4744
Sherry Sabine NewDriven@gmail.com
www.facebook.com/NewDrivenRadio
A weekly 4-hour radio show that features only independent Rock from across the US and around the world. It airs Tuesdays 8-midnight (EST). We feature independent bands from Soft Rock, Hard Rock, Punk, Metal, Southern Rock, Americana, Pop and everything in between. The first 2 hours are called New Driven Cruise and we feature the softer stuff there.

KTRL Radio
attn: Drew Slattery (Music Director), 90.5 KTRL, Box T-0095, Tarleton State U. Stephenville TX 76402
www.tarleton.edu/ktrl
A new station looking for all styles of Folk, Roots, Americana, Country and World Music.

KURT Radio
attn: Drew Slattery (Music Director), 100.7 KURT, Box T-0095, Tarleton State U. Stephenville TX 76402
www.tarleton.edu/ktrl
Send us your Rock music.

KYHY
PO Box 3422, Burbank, CA 91508
Jerry j.dailey@925thewhy.com

www.925kyhy.com
We have rocked Burbank, Los Angeles County and the World since May 1, 2008 and we continue to do so for one reason – independent music.

KRIM
500 E. Tyler Pkwy. Ste. A, Payson, AZ 85541
PH: 928-978-3795
Kit McGuire kit@krimfm.com
www.krim-fm.com
Kit McGuire is well known for presenting unsigned/Indie artists to the masses. Kit personally screens all artist's demos, media kits, promo packs, and track-by-track. Kit also screens for great music from artists hard at work touring and fulfilling their dream.

High Plains Morning - HPPR
101 W. 5th St. #100, Amarillo, TX 79101
PH: 806-367-9088
Johnny Black music@hppr.org - www.hppr.org
Singer/Songwriters, Bluegrass, Contemporary Folk, World, Jazz and much more. Includes a performance studio.

KPFK 90.7 FM
Samm Brown's "For the Record", a weekly radio program on KPFK 90.7 FM, is seeking artists/bands for airplay and critique. Each Sunday, Brown hosts a program that focuses on the entertainment industry in general and the music business in particular. Send package to Samm Brown's For the Record, KPFK Radio, 90.7 FM, 11054 Ventura Blvd. No. 237, Studio City, CA. 91604.

Radio Rietveld
Frederik Roeskestraat 96, 1076 ED Amsterdam, the Netherlands
PH: 003120-5711600 FX: 003120-5711654
Hans Kuiper/ Gijs Muller radiorietveld@gmail.com
www.radiorietveld.nl
Features independent music, originally produced programs, sounds capes, radio plays, interviews and art specials. Connected to the Gerrit Rietveld Art Academy in Amsterdam.

WBMB Baruch College Radio, 87.9 FM the Biz
55 Lexington Ave. Ste. 3-280, New York, NY 10010
PH: 646-312-4720
Gina Alioto ginanalioto@gmail.com
www.wbmbradio.com
Featuring all styles of music.

WNCW - Isothermal College
PO Box 804, Spindale, NC 28160
PH: 828-287-8000 x349 FX: 828-287-8012
Martin Anderson marting@wncw.org
www.wncw.org
We're always looking for new Americana, Rock, Singer/Songwriter and World music to play.

WOJB - Lac Courte Oreilles Ojibwa College
13386 W. Trepania Rd. Hayward, WI 54843
PH: 715-634-2100 FX: 715-634-4070
Nicky Kellar programdirector@wojb.org -
www.wojb.org
One of the most diverse and popular stations in

Wisconsin.
KRCK-FM 97.7
73-733 Fred Waring Dr. #201, Palm Desert, CA 92260
PH: 760-341-0123 FX: 760-341-7455
The Big KC kc@krck.com
http://www.krck.com
KRCK supports local talent and encourages independent artists. Rock & Alternative format.

Try these resources
Indie Bible directory

Standing for the King, While in the Spotlight of the Media

Chapter 15

How to Get Your Music on Pandora Internet Radio

There are several ways to get your music on Pandora. They are always looking for new music to play for their listeners, so they watch blogs, radio stations, show listings, charts and things like that. In addition, while they don't automatically add everything they hear. When an artist reaches a certain level of visibility they will try to make that music available on Pandora.

That's the first thing you need to know. If you are connecting with an audience or community in a strong way; if you're playing good rooms and getting attention, you will have a fine chance of getting into our collection.

They know they can't find everything, though, so for the many deserving bands that we miss for one reason or another (and for bands that are just starting out), they offer a web-based music submission process that is free and open to everyone. (Adapted from Pandora Blog)

Here's how it works:

1. Register for Pandora (the submission process is connected to listener accounts, so you can use your existing account if you have one).

2. Go to http://submitmusic.pandora.com and follow the directions for submitting.

3. If your CD meets the requirements for

submission (you have to have a valid UPC code and the record has to be for sale in the Amazon CD store), you'll be prompted to upload two songs along with any biographical or press information and any links you'd like us to know about.

4. When we get to your submission, we listen and make a decision about whether your submission is right for us. (This takes time, so be patient.)

5. If you're accepted, we send you an email with a customized mailing label that you'll use to send us your record. If we pass on your record we let you know on your submission page and we encourage you to keep us posted on your future work.[3]

Standing for the King, While in the Spotlight of the Media

Chapter 16

14 Ways to Promote Your Music Online

Make your profile page and website work harder

Computer Music Specials writes, "If you want your music to reach the wider listening world, the internet can be your best friend. However, if you're going to have a presence online, you need to make sure that you do things right."[4]

Here are MusicRadar's top tips for making an impression via the World Wide Web...

1. **Join a social network**
   MySpace and Facebook act as a one-stop band advert where you can upload anything you want: photos, songs, video, text and more. Limit yourself to two or three social networks though – you don't want to spread yourself too thinly.

2. **Set up a website**
   As good as MySpace and Facebook are, having your own website too looks more professional. Websites are cheap to host and easy to build so there are no excuses. Remember to update it as often as your social network profile though...

3. **Keep your website/profile current**
   Make sure that you post regular updates and news stories. Add new photos frequently and generally keep your profile looking busy. That way you'll be seen as a serious, enthusiastic, up-and-coming act. Regular profile/website updates will also keep things interesting for returning fans.

4. **Write a Biography**
   An artist bio should be concise, informative and interesting. People (particularly venue

staff) don't want to know that your band was formed "in the first year of uni by songwriter Joe Bloggs and producer John Smith" – cut out the background and write something that's a bit different. "As good as MySpace and its mates are, having your own website too looks more professional." *(Contact a professional if needed).*

5. **Get some good photos**
   Top-notch imagery is crucial if you want to be noticed online. Try to present a uniform 'look' that fits with your music. There are aspiring photographers who will be willing to take press or live photos of you and/or your band for little or no money. Take advantage of them!

6. **Offer your songs for free download**
   If you're an independent act, your goal is to get your music heard as much as possible. Be aware that people are much more inclined to listen if you offer the occasional track free. If you decide not to give away your music, then at least offer streaming full-length versions of your tracks rather than short clips.

7. **Interact with other artists**

Networking with other artists and bands by keeping in regular contact and giving feedback on their music means you're likely to find partners and be asked to play support slots. Musicians are also generally more interested as fans when it comes to independent music like yours.

8. **Dedicate some time to your fans**
Replying to mail and friend requests can sometimes be a chore but try to avoid blanket "thanks for the add" messages. If you keep things personal, you're far more likely to be remembered and if your audience likes you, they'll be predisposed to like your music.

9. **Avoid spamming**
While it's important to keep in touch with your fans, repeated spam is annoying, so reserve mass messaging for special events. It's far more effective to tailor your messages and gig invites to individuals or small groups of people – there's no point telling someone from Land's End that you're gigging in Dundee.

10. **Make sure social network friends are valuable**
It can be tempting to add every person you

come across, but when it comes to social networks, high profile views are what make you look good and not your friend count. Make sure you add only valuable friends who you think will like your music and visit your profile. "There's no point telling someone from Land's End that you're gigging in Dundee."

11. **Do something to stand out from the crowd**
The sad truth is that the quality of your music won't always be enough to get you noticed. Try doing a blog, a quiz, a gimmick – anything that will make your website or profile a bit different and interesting.

12. **Get a short, snappy URL**
Your website and your social network profiles will need a short snappy URL (web address) that's easy to remember. Bear in mind that you might be shouting your URL through the PA at a noisy gig to apathetic, drunken punters – keep it obvious and make sure the spelling is logical.

13. **Get your songs on iTunes**
Nothing says professionalism like having your songs available to buy on the world's largest

online music store. Websites such as CD Baby can get your tracks online for a small charge – you can then link to your songs in the store from your website/profile.

14. **Keep your social profile concise**
    There are all manner of widgets and plug-ins available for social networks, but while they may look flashy, having too many may obscure the important info on your profile. They can also make your profile slow to load – remember that people generally don't have much patience on the net.

Chapter 17

Want a Radio Interview?

Radio Guest List is a great website for registering to become a radio guest. Get radio interviews and podcast publicity guest's interview bookings free! Free radio, Internet radio, satellite radio, talk radio, podcast and TV talk show guest expert's interviews booking service.

Post your information or publicity online.

http://www.radioguestlist.com

Radio Guest List is the #1 free radio guest, podcast, talk radio, Internet radio, satellite radio and TV talk show guest expert interview booking service!

Chapter 18

How to Prepare for TV

One of the areas the King will call you to minister is television. It is important that you walk out your season of preparation so that you are ready when television starts calling on you. Everyone in ministry or business wants to be on television, but not everyone can actually get on television. If you are true and dedicated, with motivation and persistence you can go after your dream. Follow these tips in order to secure a spot on television.

Get an agent or manager.
- Agents or managers know the ins and outs of the television industry. They can help you get your foot in the door. An agent can also help coach you about things you should and shouldn't do to get a booked on a television show.

Have headshots taken.
- It is important to have current, professional headshots taken, because they can make or break your chances of getting a call for a television appearance. Headshots are the television show's first impression of you and they should represent who you are and display your versatility as an artist, actor or minister. Update your photos every couple of years so that reflect you in your current place in life.

Attend casting calls.
- Many television shows and commercials host open casting calls that anyone off the streets can attend. Be Prepared! As much as possible with the information you are given about the part. Be open to criticism, because it can only help you during your next audition.

Research what shows are taping in your area.
- Do your homework. Shows that are taping in your area may need a variety of guests at any given time. Having local a door open to a major television show has the potential to give you a big boost into the television scene.

Be open-minded.
- Remember that appearing on television is like anything -- you have to start at the bottom. Take any opportunities that give you exposure without compromising your character and integrity. Remember, you are there to represent the King.

Standing for the King, While in the Spotlight of the Media

Chapter 19

How to Get Coverage In Print Media

Contacting with the media is not as difficult as you might think. Whether or not your project will make the news often depends on the initial contact and the impact you make. In this section, we will look at the best way of communicating with print media, including newspapers and magazines.

The best and most common way of communicating with the media – print, radio and

TV – is through preparing and distributing a **media release**. A media release is also known as a press release or a news release. A media release is a document containing the message you want to convey. It takes a particular format, which is changed only slightly, depending on the nature of your ministry.

How to Build Your Media Release

Your media release should include:
- Your business name and logo at the top.
- Your contact details near the top.
- The date.
- An attention-grabbing heading.
- The information formatted into individual short paragraphs, with the most interesting information summarized in the first paragraph.
- Background information about yourself and/or your business or ministry at the conclusion of the media release with its own heading.
- Always check for spelling and grammar. If

your media release contains grammatical and spelling errors, it becomes impossible to read and you loose your professional image.

Your media release needs to answer the following questions where applicable. Keep the following in mind when creating it:

- **What** – is it about, what's happening?
- **When** – is the event taking place or when did it happen?
- **Where** – is this national or local? Where is the location?
- **Who** – are the key people and the business involved?
- **How** – what are the details?

Finally, the following tips will go a long way in helping you get your message into the hands of the media.

- Always write in the subject line of your email what the media release subject matter.
- Write in the body of your email the subject matter of the attached media release.

- Don't send large attachments.
- Never send them an image with the first email and media release.
- Give them your contact details in the email and make sure you are available.
- Give them what they need for their story.
- Don't ever mention the advertising dollars you may have spent with the publication.
- Exclusive means exclusive.
- Don't send them garbage.

Chapter 20

Got A Press Kit? What's a Press Kit?

What is a Press Kit? Answer. Press kits, also called media kits, are promotional materials that are put together to help get your company, group or organization noticed. In other words, it provides information about your ministry, group or company. What is needed in an Artist Press Kit?

Artist Statement
The **artist statement** is a written summary about your art, and the direction you are going. It

articulates what your art is about, so that others will know where you stand as an artist or minister. Artist statements should be updated often, especially before exhibitions and explorations of new themes. Most artists already have one of these, so there should be no problem formatting and editing it for your press kit.

Artist Biography
The biography is about what you have accomplished as an artist. It highlights your exhibitions, awards, achievements, etc. The main difference between this and an artist statement is statements are written in first person, while biographies are generally third person. It is also information, which most artists already have complied.

Artist Resume
The artist's resume typically has the same

structure as a regular employment resume. It is a summary of an artist's contact information, education, exhibitions, awards and more.

Artist Business Cards

Business cards brand the artist with a professional image and are effective for promotional purposes. Include your logo, your name (or studio name) and contact information. Also, include your artist website if you have one. Keep business cards with you at all times and include at least one in your press package.

Press Releases

Press releases are summaries sent to media outlets regarding your ministry and other events. Include any recent and important press releases to your media kit.

Published articles

Published articles can include write-ups about

you or your ministry.

A photo of yourself
Make sure you have professionally photographed headshots.

Keep in mind, that you can create an electronic press kit through companies such as Sonic Bids. It will save money in the long run.

Chapter 21

Let the Vision Speak

Habakkuk 2:2-3 gives us a road map for waiting on the vision to come to pass:

> *And the Lord answered me and said, Write the vision and engrave it so plainly upon tablets that everyone who passes may [be able to] read [it easily and quickly] as he hastens by. For the vision is yet for an appointed time and it hastens to the end [fulfillment]; it will not deceive or disappoint. Though it tarry, wait*

[earnestly] for it, because it will surely come; it will not be behindhand on its appointed day.

Write the vision for your ministry or business so that it is clear to you. Remember, you may be the only one who sees or believes in the vision, but it is important that you see it before anyone else. Never allow dream killers, dream stealers or dream haters to cause you to abort or mis-carry your dream:

- ➤ The vision should be engraved on your heart and on paper so that you can remain focused on it.

- ➤ You can't run with a vision you can't see. It is equivalent of trying to run in the dark.

- ➤ The vision has an appointed time - God's

time.

- ➤ The enemy wants you to procrastinate when it comes to the vision. Procrastination is a key element in vision abortions.

- ➤ The vision will come to pass as long as you have committed it to the Lord.

- ➤ The vision will not come through deception or lies; it must be birthed out in spirit and in truth.

- ➤ Even when it seems as though the vision is stalled, dead or delayed, wait for it because is has an appointed time of release and it will come to pass.

Finally, your vision is not designed to destroy you; it is there to strengthen you. Regardless of what the vision looks like today, know that it is a grand design of God that will bring Him glory. Allow the King to build the house and it will stand and withstand every attack of the enemy. It will thrive and grow in every area. The vision will speak and when it speaks, please be ready.

Get in alignment for the assignment that God has for you, so that you receive the advancement in the Kingdom agenda.

Alignment + Assignment = Advancement

Chapter 22

Are Your Ready to Minister for the King?

Are you ready to go out and minister for the King? Are you ready to take a stand and proclaim a message to a dying world? The only thing I can add at this point is to make sure you are "walking the walk" on and off the stage.

Your music or ministry should be an instrument to deliver your message. The most important element of your performance is your ministry. The Christian music arena is in need of a fresh anointing. Christian artists can now develop a ministry and be free to express their talent at the same time. You should not have to sell out in order to have your message heard. As a Kingdom Priest, you have two choices:

✓ Your can minister FOR the King.
Or
✓ You can minister FOR the world.

What is the difference? When you are a minister FOR the King, you **minister** according to the pattern set by the King. When you minister FOR the world, you **perform** according to the pattern set by the world.

It is time that we take a firm stand on the strength of God's Word and walk as a Kingdom Priest with a Kingdom mindset and a Kingdom Agenda. The time for compromise is over. It is time to take your stand like modern day Gideon's in an arena where there may only be a handful of soldiers standing with you. Alternatively, you may be a modern day Shamgar and destroy a host of demonic forces with only a stick (Judges 3:31). Whatever your mandate, stand firm and see the power of God, the Koach power: (*vigor, strength, force, capacity, power, wealth, means or substance. Generally, it means "capacity" or "ability"*) move in your life like never before.

If I called on you today to appear on television, radio, print media or a live performance, would you be ready? It very well could happen, remember God has graced me with the ability to flow in each of those arenas. Would you have your "I's dotted and your "T's" crossed? Or would you have to make excuses as to why you were unable to make the engagement. Would you wish that you had purchased this book or another similar to it? Would you have to go back to the drawing board and regroup?

If you are not ready, it is okay, because today is the day that you take your gift serious and begin preparing to minister for the King. Today is the day that you get your act together and begin looking and living like the Kingdom Priest that you are. Today is also that you begin developing the strategies necessary to make it in ministry or business. Please know that your looks, gifts and talents will only take you so far, it will be your character, integrity and your ability to stand and withstand, that will keep you there.

Commit your plans to God in prayer and allow Him to build the house for you. Lay everything, thoughts, hopes or dreams on the altar before

Him and allow Him to lead and guide you. Don't get caught up in the hype and enthusiasm, it's a recipe for disaster. The building process can be long and arduous, but in the end, it will succeed.

Follow God's plan for success in your ministry, business and life. Success comes knocking on the doors of those who are prepared and equipped to open the door. **Are you ready?**

Standing for the King, While in the Spotlight of the Media

Appendix
The Budget Process - Expenses

STUDIO BUDGET
Producer Advance Fee _____
Studio Time   _____
Overdubs   _____
Lead vocals   _____
Background vocals   _____
Misc. Time   _____
      TOTAL STUDIO _____

DUPLICATION BUDGET
Cover Design   _____
Photography   _____
Graphic Artist   _____
CD Duplication   _____
Mastering   _____
      TOTAL DUPL. _____

TALENT COST
Lead Musicians   _____
Musicians (4)   _____
Overdubs   _____
Background Singers   _____
Choir   _____
Engineer   _____
Lead Singers   _____
      TOTAL TALENT _____

MARKETING BUDGET
Press Release   _____
CD Release Party   _____
Radio Promotions   _____
Electronic Press Kit   _____
Traditional Press Kits _____
TV Commercials   _____
Social Media   _____
Website Design   _____
Poster\Flyer\Postcard   _____

TOTAL MARKET _____

TOURING BUDGET
Hotels   _____
Vehicles   _____
Food   _____
Clothing   _____
Travel
(Airline, bus, etc.) _____

TOTAL TOURING _____

NOTES ON BUDGETING: Always take into consideration additional studio time might be needed. Therefore, instead of budgeting for 2 hours, budget 4 hours. It is better to be under budget than over budget and run short of funding.

About the Author

God has called Jacquie Hadnot to encourage, inspire, motivate and activate the gifts of the Spirit in order to raise powerful ministries in the body of Christ. She is becoming a voice on the subject of prayer, worship and spiritual warfare.

She is recognized as a modern-day apostle with a strong prophetic and psalmist anointing. She has a revelational teaching ministry with a mandate to saturate the world with the Word of God. Jacquie's heart is to see people arise and walk in the destiny and inheritance of the Lord.

She founded and established It Is Written Ministries, a publication company, an accounting and consulting firm, and a global radio station. As a retired accountant and financial executive,

Jacquie blends ministerial and entrepreneurial applications in her ministry to enrich and empower a diverse audience with skills and abilities to take kingdoms for the Lord Jesus Christ. A lecturer, conference speaker, transformational teacher, business trainer, and financial consultant, she provides consulting services to businesses, churches, and individuals. She has written over twenty-five books, manuals, and other materials on intimacy with God, prayer, fasting and spiritual warfare. She has also released several music Cds and received numerous music and book publishing awards.

Beyond the pulpit, Jacquie is a talk-show host on both television and radio with her own programs, The Exchange, a television talk show and Light for Your Path, a radio-teaching ministry. Weekly she applies God's wisdom to today's world solutions. Her ministry goal is to make Christ's teachings relevant for today. She also publishes a quarterly magazine.

In addition to her vast experience, Jacquie has a Th.d. in Pastoral Theology and a Masters in Ministry Leadership/Education. She is also a wife, mother of one daughter and grandmother of one grandson. She and her husband, Gregory presently pastor It Is Written Ministries in Kansas City Kansas. They also serve as owners and officers of Igniting the Fire Media Group.

Standing for the King, While in the Spotlight of the Media

Other Books & Materials by Dr. Jacquie

Books in Print

- The Art of Spiritual Warfare: Strategies for Effective Warfare
- There's A Famine in the Land: *Overcoming Great Recession*
- Your Declaration of Dependence on God
- Closing the Doors to Satan's Attacks: *Overcoming Fear*
- Trapped in the Arms of Death: *Overcoming Grip of Suicide*
- The Extravagant Love of God: Experiencing the Prophetic Flow
- Cry Aloud, Spare Not! A Prophetic Call to Fast God Has Chosen
- Cry Aloud, Spare Not! The Companion-Study Guide
- His Mercy Endures Forever: Psalms, Prayers & Meditations
- To Make War with the Saints; Satan's Kingdom Agenda
- A Treasure in the Pleasure of Loving God
- Loving God through His Names: 365 Days of the Year
- Where Is Your God? Have We Lost Referential Fear of the Lord?

Booklets

- When Fear Crept In
- Deeper…
- Naked, Broken and Unashamed

Standing for the King, While in the Spotlight of the Media

Audio Books & Teachings
- More of You... (Volume 1)
- In the Face of Adversity: *Overcoming Life's Storms*
- Be Not Deceived...
- Where Is Your God?
- Recognizing Your Due Season
- Praying the Healing Scriptures
- The Enemy in Me: *Overcoming Self-Life Issues*
- Trusting God in a Season of Discouragement
- The Harlot Heart

Music
- The Extravagant Love of God
- The Spoken Word of Love
- His Mercy Endures Forever: Praying the Psalms

DVD
- When Your Faith is Being Tested
- What Made David Run
- Agents of Change
- Virtuous Women of Worship

TO CONTACT DR. JACQUIE:
www.jacquiehadnot.com
www.ignitingthefire.net
Or write us:
jacquie@jacquiehadnot.com

NOTES

Standing for the King, While in the Spotlight of the Media

Standing for the King, While in the Spotlight of the Media

Standing for the King, While in the Spotlight of the Media

Looking for a Ministry of Kings & Priests?

Looking for sound information on the industry of media? Want to know what a Kingdom Priest looks like? Looking for a way to grow your ministry dimensionally? Stuck in a relentless cycle of hype that leads to nowhere? Contact the Kingdom Media Foundation and discover what it means to follow the King's agenda.

Informative and insightful, the Kingdom Media Foundation is a ministry of Kingdom Priests with a Kingdom mindset for the Kingdom agenda.

Consider attending the annual Kingdom Media Festival. Visit the website for more information on the annual gathering of Priests and Kings.

Kingdom Media Foundation
P.O Box 1527
Sumter, SC 29151
803 775-7605

www.kingdommusicfamily.com

Resources

[1] Greg Skinner, Songwriting FAQs.
[2] <u>Indie Bible directory</u>
[3] Pandora Radio
[4] Computer Music Specials, November 13, 2008, 14:51 GMT

Standing for the King, While in the Spotlight of the Media

www.ingramcontent.com/pod-product-compliance
Lightning Source LLC
Chambersburg PA
CBHW071123090426
42736CB00012B/1995